Religions
of the World

By Sushmita Kirkland
Art by Ilya Fortuna

Dedication:

This book is dedicated to all the curious kids of this world as they grow into adults loving our beautiful world. This book is also dedicated to my little family.

Sushmita Kirkland

© 2021 Sushmita Kirkland; illustrated by Ilya Fortuna

All rights reserved.

This book or any portion thereof may not be reproduced or used in any manner whatsoever without the express written permission of the publisher except for the use of brief quotations in a book review or scholarly journal.

First Printing: 2021
ISBN 978-1-7371337-8-0
Publishing company: KirklandPublishing

Hi friends, I am Kai, and I am Keanu
We love to learn and share what we know
We are going on another trip around the world
Learning about religions of the world

Before we go on our trip
Do you know what religion is?
It was not so easy for us to explain
It took many questions and answers for us to learn

Our mommy says it is the relationship between
something that we can't see or hear
But you and only you, can feel
some call this GOD
some call it UNIVERSE
and others call it ENERGY
Just like the connection we have with mom and our dad
Just like the one you have with your family
It might be different from that of ours
But the relationship is still special and just yours
There are so many types of religions in this world
Each unique and special to those that most need
Let's go explore and learn

HINDUISM

The sacred sound Om

Hinduism on the map

Our first stop today is mom's place of birth
The country we love and the traditions we respect
We are going to India
Most people in India are Hindu's
Hindus are those who practice Hinduism
Hindus have not one, not two
But 33 million gods they pray to

There is the elephant god Ganesh who loves sweet
There is the god Shiva, who can destroy a bad guy like a superhero
There is the dancing god Nataraja, who loves to dance
There is the goddess Lakshmi, who is brings lots of money and fortune
The biggest Hindu festival is called 'Diwali' which means "rows of lighted lamps"
We celebrate by decorating our home with lamps called 'Diyas' and other colorful lights
Dazzling fireworks go off, creating a spectacle of noise and lights
This helps to scare away evil spirits and celebrate the victory of good over evil
In Hinduism, they believe God is inside every soul
So next time you are mad at someone
Remember there is God in all of us
Even the ones that make us a little mad

ISLAM

Islam on the map

Our next stop from India is Indonesia
Why did we go to Indonesia you ask?
Indonesia has the most number of Muslims in the world
Muslims connect with their god through Islam
Unlike the Hindus, they do not have many gods
Islam was shared with the world through a prophet

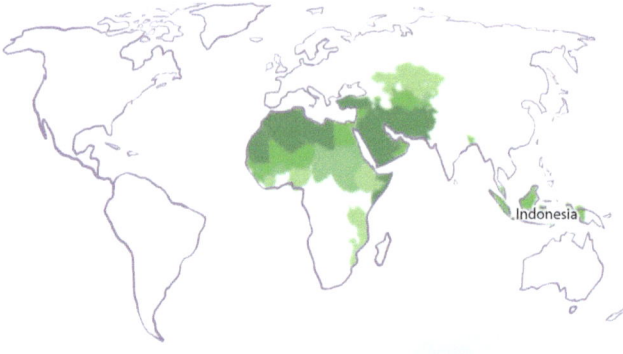

What is a Prophet you say?
A smart man that knows a lot about a lot
The prophet is called Muhammad
He said one true connection for Muslims is to Allah
Allah is the God they connect to
Muslims believe in being kind and sharing with others
Muslims read all about Allah through the holy Quran
They also spend a whole month of every year fasting
Do you know what fasting is?
Well, they do not eat from sunrise to sunset
Not even a tiny treat or a sip of water
We think that is pretty amazing
Don't you?

CHRISTIANITY

Our next stop from here is the United States
Why did we go to the United States?
Well firstly, because we are Americans, and we live here
Also, America has the most number of Christians
Who are Christians, you say?
It is another religion that is practiced around the world
Christians believe and connect to God through Jesus Christ
Some also pray to the mother of Jesus, whose name is Mary

Christianity on the map

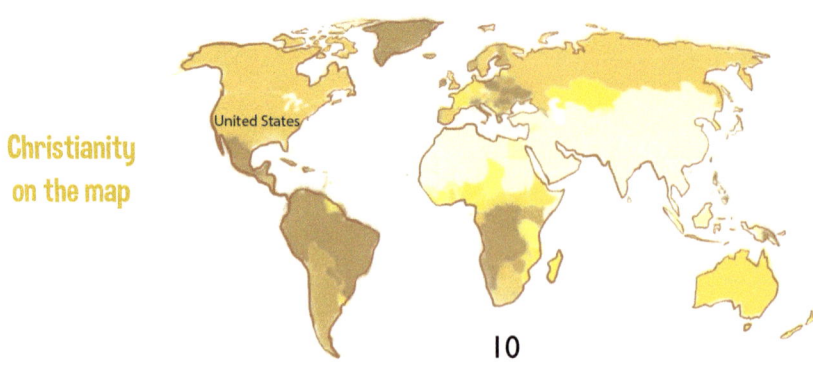

Christians also believe that one God created heaven, earth, and the universe
Christians read all about their god through the holy Bible
Christmas is the celebration of the birth of Jesus
All the kids around the world love Christmas
As we get gifts from Santa and his helpers
Now remember to be good and listen to your mom and dad
For you will not be on the good list for gifts and
We don't want you to be sad

JUDAISM

Star of David

Judaism on the map

Our next stop is in Israel
Israel is home to a lot of people who follow Judaism
Israel is also home to Muslims, Christians, and even Hindus
The people who follow Judaism are Jewish
Jewish people believe and connect to just one God
They call their god Yahweh
They also believe God is not a person
But God is everywhere, God is one

Jewish people visit the Synagogue to worship and connect with their community
What is a community you say?
It is all the people that we live together with
The teachers of Judaism are called Rabbis
One of the biggest festivals celebrated in Judaism is called Hannukah
For eight nights, candles are lit in a menorah
Families play games, sing songs, and exchange gifts
They also recite special blessings and prayers
Shabbat is the Jewish day of Rest
It begins before sunset on Friday night and lasts until late Saturday
They read all about God in their holy book called Torah
Did you know you can't touch the Torah out of respect?
That's right, readers use a special pointer called a Yad
We think that is pretty cool and rad

← Dreidel to win sweets

← Hanukkah sweets

BUDDHISM

Dharmachakra

Judaism on the map

Our next stop is China
China is home to the greatest number of people
who follow Buddhism
What is Buddhism you say?
Some say it is a way of life
While others say it is a religion
Either way we want to explore more
Share what we know
The Buddha taught how to live a life
That is without any pain and suffering
Buddhists believe you can be happy in life
If you don't always want things and offering(s)
I don't quite understand is what you say?

Let us explain a little more in play
You always want to buy more toys
But the more toys you have, you keep wanting more
Instead, try giving some to your friends or those who have none
We love the idea of sharing what we have
Don't you?
Our parents always say life is about love and not things
We think that is what Buddha wants you to remember

These are just some of the religions of the world
There are many more religions around the globe
We hope you will ask your mommies and daddies to teach you about them
When we meet again you can tell us about them

We enjoyed traveling the world
Sharing what we learned
Religion is many things to many of us
One thing we learned from it all is
Religion is being kind
Religion is sharing and caring
Religion is believing you will get home
Even if you are lost

Until next time friends
Never stop exploring!

About the Author

Sushmita Kirkland is a Diversity, Equity and Inclusion strategist who wants to show the world about educating children about belonging and inclusion through exposure to the world and its many cultures. Sushmita is in the process of creating a series based on the concept of culture and belonging for kids between the ages of 1-7.

 Connect the religious symbols using arrows similar to the arrow you can see in the Nativity scene

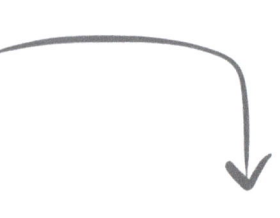

CHRISTIANITY

HINDUISM

ISLAM

JUDAISM

BUDDHISM

Let's color our beautiful planet in rainbow colors

www.ingramcontent.com/pod-product-compliance
Lightning Source LLC
Chambersburg PA
CBHW061402090426
42743CB00002B/117